The Cop Who Rides Alone

The Cop Who Rides Alone

and other poems
by Ross Martin

Zoo Press

I wish to thank the editors of the following publications in which these poems, sometimes in different forms, first appeared:

Agni: "Plants Move"; *Big Bridge*: "Sitting in the Sun"; *Bomb*: "Signatures," "Making Believe," "Basketball with the Methodists"; *Boulevard*: "The Parkmoor Diner Has Fake Eggs"; *Denver Quarterly*: "Oh, And…," "Someone Says Draw You," "Frotteur"; *Fence*: "Alone in Our Place"; *Jewish Spectator*: "Naked Light Over Sleeping Water," "To Heidegger"; *Kenyon Review*: "Reading Bibles in Tennessee," "It Is Late But Not Too"; *Lit*: "From Our Cottage, by B. Blake," "Vicarious," "First Person," "Helio Me"; *Maisonneuve*: "A Fish," "Fourth Person," "Memorial Day Night," "We're Famous"; *Many Mountains Moving*: "My Father Slow Motioning," "View from My Gym"; *Nebraska Review*: "Dividing My Father," "Icetrap"; *Phoebe*: "Before You Marry Someone Else, in California"; *Pleiades*: "Apocalypses," "[Memorize what you are…]," "My Heart Goes Out to You"; *Prairie Schooner*: "New Jersey Mother," "Ossuary," "Conversation Piece"; *Slope*: "The World According to Dad," "Men's Room Barnard"; *Verse Press* (Young American Poets Feature): "The Cop Who Rides Alone," "No One Eats in the Chinese Restaurant No One Eats In," "Being Charles Nelson Reilly"; *Witness* (Crime In America Issue): "Have You Seen Me." "Icetrap" was reprinted in *Big Bridge*; "From Our Cottage, by B. Blake" was featured on Poetry Daily.

Thank you Vermont Studio Center, Neil Azevedo, Olga Broumas, Jeremy Countryman, Spike Lee, Yusef Komunyakaa, Eric Pankey, the One Fish Gang Collective, David Lehman, Derek Webster, Paula Roy, Mark Bibbins. Thank you Erin Belieu, for everything. Most importantly, I thank my family.

Zoo Press • P.O. Box 22990 • Lincoln, Nebraska 68542
Printed in the United States of America

Produced and designed for Zoo Press by Compass Books • Minneapolis • Sioux Falls
Cover by Scott Stoel © 2001 • Cover photo "Bob Lopez" © Bernie Munk

Library of Congress Cataloging-in-Publication Data
    Martin, Ross, 1973-
      The cop who rides alone/ by Ross Martin.
        p.   cm.
      ISBN: 0-9708177-1-1
      1. Title.
      PS3613.A785 C67 2001
      811'.6--DC21

c 10 9 8 7 6 5 4 3 2 1

FIRST EDITION

— for Jordana

Contents

[Memorize what you are...]   3

i

From Our Cottage, by B. Blake   7
Apocalypses   9
Helio Me   10
Basketball with the Methodists   11
Dividing My Father   13
Memorial Day Night   14
Years Since You've Seen Me   15
Love Your Cousin   16
My Heart Goes Out to You   17
Vicarious   18
My Father, Slow Motioning   19
First Person   20
Dispatch Her   21
Stained Glass Wedding   22
Conversation Piece   24
Sitting in the Sun   25
New Jersey Mother   26
"The World According to Dad"   27

Icetrap   31
Reading Bibles in Tennessee   32
Aminals   33
Memorial to Horrible Friend   35
New York City Is the Capitol of the World   36
Frotteur   37
Men's Room, Barnard   38
The Man with No Children   39
Radio: 4:01pm: 9 July   40
The Parkmoor Diner Has Fake Eggs   41
The Cop Who Rides Alone   42
No One Eats in the Chinese Restaurants No One Eats In   44
View from My Gym   45
Fools for the Danger of This Woman   47
It Is Late But Not Too   48
You Are Her New Lover   49
Before You Marry Someone Else, in California   50
Reconsidering   51
My Woman   52
We're Famous   53
Everything Is Always About You   54
I Love You During Dinner   55
What to Do with the Ring   56
Telling   58
Alone in Our Place   59
Signals   60
Making Believe   61
Someone Says Draw You   62
Blame It on Division   63
Worship   64

iii

Fourth Person   68
Dedications   69
Making Tea   70
Dinoflagella   71
A Fish   73
If You Stood You Would Not Fall   74
Have You Seen Me   75
Plants Move   77
Naked Light Over Sleeping Water   79
To Heidegger   80
Letter Home from Barcelona   81
Richard Lindner's Cast   82
My Eyes and Benicio del Toro's   84
Poem for Míklos Radnóti   85
Being Charles Nelson Reilly   86
Oh, and...   88
Ossuary   89
You Return from Your Daily Walk   90

*At first he had decided he must find a solution and an
explanation for the problems of existence, or he must shoot
himself. But he had done neither one thing nor the other.*

Tolstoy, *Anna Karenina*

[Memorize what you are...]

Memorize what you are, for your own sake.
This is the mouth that is late to your ear.
Raw materials are available.
Do not begin here.
Within uncertainty be the enormous.
People have been killed.
Begin between two thunders.
None of the names will change.
This is the only way to tell it:

From Our Cottage, by B. Blake

Dear Good Friend to Whom I am Somehow Indebted,

There is a new fruit popped up in our garden!
Your plate is late but *I am working again!*An avocado's the
    most like
my wife's sex I Can't go into it

right now. No future Distractions
on the Horizon.Remember when I wrote you *My wife is like a
    flame of many colours of*
precious jewels?
Disregard as False poetry! I have begun to work again! Sorry
the plate's not done yet I been busy with
the place. I know,

I know I'm Late.Things are together, though, you can Count
    on that.

Least this letters in certain terms.
Dont want to mince *Did I tell you I have begun to work and*
*find that I can work with greater pleasure than ever. And tho the
    weather is wet,*

the Air is very Mild. much milder than it was in London when
    My
Wife *Our cottage looks more and more beautiful.* So does
wife. *I have been absorbed*

by of all peopl *Milton, Homer and Spenser.* of course and
the very idea of my wife's thighs in no Breeze at al. *Deliteful*

study!Speaking of which have I told you about
the little Grl I found
lost, coverd in the chimney Sweep's

soot? *I have begun to work* on a poem bout her. Great
    GoodLord!*My fingers*
Emit sparks of fire with Expectation of my future labours!

*Nothing is necessary to me but to do my*Wife says hello as well
    and
joins me in everlasting apology
for the Delay in engraving...
                                Ever Yours Sincerely,
                                B.B.

ps I must admit a problem these days reconciling
    Drive your cart and your plow over the bones of the dead
                                        and

            The cut worm forgives the plow.
They dont make go d bedfellows.

pps Have you ever even to meet *Catherine*, my belovd wife?

Apocalypses

Pointless, Pointless were Lee Harvey Oswald's last words,
I think, or maybe someone else's
who killed someone more
or less important. I can't remember

where I was
when anybody died.

When Marlon Brando dies he always
says the same perfect thing:
The Horror, The Horror.

Sometimes I say that
out loud. No one is around.
I don't know where I am.
And I can never remember the last time
I died, where I was.

Helio Me

In the
smallest
hour

of
the day
we save

light
I am
no more

myself
than
the green

I green
into
another

year
God
let me

sleep
through
this

hour
as we
repeat it

Basketball with the Methodists

This steeple's got dirt under the fingernails.
        —Ralph Ellison, *Juneteenth*

Here's
the roof,
here's the steeple,
open it up and see all
the people, crosses worn
proud under colored mesh, dipped
in silver but never removed, and me
I am here, the Jew that Wes brought along.

Shoot
the rock!
Shoot the rock!
the Methodists shout,
and a rock is a stone and
stones are thrown and someone
threw stones at Jesus, once, but who?
is the answer to the ultimate question, so
I shoot the ball and it falls asleep on the tired, red rim…

we
wait,
wait for it
to pop in or out,
and it's up there still,
a binary prayer, no need
for guilt, bottomless despair.
When the preacher peeks in his pious
head he's sure he sees in his men moves God
must have put there when they were born. These

are
the men
of peripheral
vision, troops of hoops,
straight ears of the Word, cornfield
boys, tall as God's knees, the blond summer
flesh of choirgirl dreams, who lower their heads,
stretch their legs and pray, day after day is done. I know

Wes
right now
in Tennessee
must be down on his knees,
praying to air I don't go to hell
from here, Apt 1A, a Jew from Jersey,
born in Saint Barnabas without his Jesus,
like a ball without air in a steeple without people Amen.

Dividing My Father

This rare bird stamp is mine.
It doubles as a hunting license, you said.

The hunters will be surprised
one turned up in the home of a Jewish pharmacist
who never shot a gun
except that one time in the Arizona desert.

And I get the plaid pajamas, too,
and the ragged sweaters.

I'll dust off the baseball cards
and file them in a fireproof cabinet.

And the fat pharmacist figurines.

There's nothing else I can think of,
unless you've been collecting
things I don't know about.

Memorial Day Night

Long after brick after brick is laid
to rest in mortar, the Old Guard
patrols honor, the Downtown
Committee keeps sidewalks
clean, our parents keep records,
the mayor declares days…

we sit and we watch, pretending
there's action on colonial streets
on a Friday night, get bored,
drive
home past
the cemetery as it expands.

Years Since You've Seen Me

The man who in the men's room
wants so badly to look down
to the right—resists, resists,
does.

That man knows
what you know. He wants
me, piss and all.

Maybe he'll take his seat on the plane
and write about my cock
in his journal, maybe
sketch it.

Like you, I suppose, somewhere
reminding yourself, over and over,
you really did

you really did
have me
memorized for a while.

Love Your Cousin

leave your cousin
let him have
the Newark streets

what he'll do
in older men's
basements with

a *panzerfaust*
kiss and a needle
that sears

fags to shins
ribs and ash
empty

as memory
of another
man's hair

the blatant skin
chipping
skin and a

bayonet face
no one will name
a flower for.

* *panzerfaust*: tank fist (German)

My Heart Goes Out to You

Don't just sit there
write the person
you know suffering most

sincerely meaningfully
say you wish more
than anything this gloomy

Friday sitting at your desk
like a torso
you could be there

look at you you
and your knack
for identifying the face

contusion makes you
haven't spoken in
so long

why not
remember a poem
is not a poem

without something
pretty make
someone's suffering pretty.

Vicarious

Then just before I'm
born he attaches live
wires, one to each of
his nipples, and lives.

Then an assistant shoots
him in the arm with a .22
to see what it feels like.
I take the car down Route 22

past strip malls my eyes
already know, and turn
them into poems that will
not move. Take U-turns

through Jersey at the speed
of the foot on my leg.

for Chris Burden

My Father, Slow Motioning

Doesn't it all look so much more,
more—
a silver ball marbling
down the lane of crisp whispers
towards a mouth of white teeth;
the pestle's muscled crush of a pill
into powder; my mother coaxing dough
up when we don't look;
my father loving my mother.

Or is it now that I have more
time to watch him,
this slowly, the more I see how he does it.

First Person

An ant
solitary in a field
of buffalo clover

is a ganglion
not going anywhere.
But four

together
circling a dead moth on a path,
propping the food up,

there, at work,
is an idea.

What I love is
plural,
breaths held

together,
the stains of crushed bugs
not on our fingers.

Dispatch Her

The day after the night
my sister kissed her New
Jersey cop beneath a flume

and the moon at Point Pleasant
beach, she couldn't escape
her own night stick jokes

as they made out under cover,
two walkie-talkies, two
bodies loud with selfsame

sound, while outside the
summer became the winter,
nights of crows toed her

heart's frozen lawn,
all his weapons for
the time being concealed.

Stained Glass Wedding

Jesus, yellow,
  up too long,
    won't stop staring

at believers under
  the jawbone
    of a sharp donkey

that killed ten thousand.
  Think of Sampson,
    blood on blood,

blind to each death star's
  soft spot.
    The one above

the one below
  never showed
    lovers where

vulnerability is,
  how much to touch
    what is soft,

when to lie
  down, when to rise,
    so here are the wasteful

fingers, hands the right
  shape of reverent,
    distance the scar

between Sacred
     and His scared
          faithful, the glass

over a jar of sun-
     stained butterflies
          for whom nothing

but abundance
     is enough.

Conversation Piece

Open the first
page to the fat
man, red fedora
on his sleeping

dog, and another
man, probably
his son, behind
him like another dog.

Terrible wallpaper says
miserable family.

O we're perceptive,
recognizing pain
by its photogenesis.

Remind me why
I picked the album
of my dead

neighbor from the
dumpster in the
first place, put it on
the coffee table,
showed it to you.

Sitting in the Sun

On summer Sundays
at Nomahegan Swim Club
people know us.

People know us,
and when they pass our cabana
they begin to say hello.

They begin to say hello
because we've belonged
for nineteen years.
I'm not sure why.

No one's allowed on the high dive
because someone's daughter fell off and needed
reconstructive facial surgery.
We sit in the sun a lot.

New Jersey Mother

Mother folds laundry the wrong way
but won't stop

because it's not the wrong way. I rewrite
other people's love

poems. Everyone I know
is on the same Bat-channel

closing their eyes
when Batman drives us to the Batcave

so we won't remember the way
after which I hold my mouth open

every Monday for the orthodontist. Waiting
at home is a bowl of twizzlers and

no good movies.
On Oneida Street the cicadas slip off

aluminum trees. Someone and his son
are mowing our lawn.

Greg and his mother's white gloves
direct imaginary traffic.

Mother drives past him
with her eyes closed.

"The World According to Dad"

Now open your heart and get ready to take
a little journey with my daughter and me.
    —Constantine M. Mantis

Studies show college bred girls
are far more likely to have oral and
anal sex something her dad wants
nothing to do with thank you never
heard such a thing and who the hell
am I how dare I disrupt him signing
his book the whole hundred eighty
pages a letter written to his daughter
"My Shannon" she couldn't be here
tonight dad has no idea where she is
or with whom *so put on your shoes*
and go out and get 'em dear Shannon
you busy bee on a balmy campus oh
come on dad it's not all that bad maybe
she really isn't that kind of girl just
consider my wife she's got a Master's
and our daughter's going for a PhD.

Icetrap

Inside the heavy tents
on Lake Winnebago, beside cars parked

on the frozen water, the sons of Appleton
sleep to the pulpy smell from paper mills

while their fathers, who've talked about
everything there is to talk about, talk

about the Packers' first round draft options.
Back in Appleton, the roar of the Fox River

can't convince anyone of a way out.
If you listen you can hear

Bob Buchannan's famous declaration: *I've seen the future,
and it's paper.* Some waters are frozen

and some are not. The Harry Houdini Museum
is a big place and hard to get out of. Young girls dream

of Harry finding them in a lonely corridor.
Harry begs them to follow him, and they do,

to a place of no winters, where no one's father
makes paper. Where no one's father is unable

to find his way
after too many absinthes at The Harry Houdini Lounge.

Where no car sleeps on ice. Where sons
don't icefish, daughters aren't stuck home

waiting. Like fish
paved over by winter.

Reading Bibles in Tennessee

Because there is faith they will be replaced
I take Bibles
from motel rooms
and steal cheap
souvenirs from towns that remind us to keep Jesus
in our summer plans.

Because Bibles fit in moth holes
they sometimes find their way
past clouds in piles
of clothes on tractors,
and it looks like they're going
slower than they are.

There are reasons each tractor is eventually abandoned
like there are reasons fugitives settle
anonymously
in Tennessee,
like there are reasons for the distant brushfires
that char hawks.

But interconnectedness is a silly concept
when considering Bible editions,
or typos, or fugitives
watching the same TV cop
show simultaneously
across mid-western trailer parks.

There's no reason why, for example, ferocious
engines follow ferocious engines on highways,
crops obey a contagious
regimen, Bible
stories are read and forgotten like
the ones before.

Aminals

Tuesday, family
day at the Saint Louis
Zoo, a good time

to go if you have young
children age three
to ten. Elephants

pee popcorn yellow,
sweep their hay where
they want it to go,

fake smirks
to get the flashes
over with. Kids

are kids, blow
their noses,
feed popcorn to

llamas wish
they had more.
Week after week

no one suspects
my girlfriend's aunt,
a can of Pabst in her

flower dress,
half-cocked beside
the white chickens,

who gives no hint,
lunatic eyes,
just swigs

the Pabst
and knocks
your son down

on the pavement
with a kick of
her leg, just

when your daughter
asks you where
aminals come from.

Memorial to Horrible Friend

we don't harbor the slow virus…
        —Miroslav Holub

We aren't the Zoroastrians of Persia.
We don't mount his dead flesh
here, Brooklyn, New York,

high on a far dakhma,
vulture sun to claw
the empty meat of apology.

We just stand beside the rest.
We tear off a piece of our neck ties,
pin the shreds to our buttondowns.

We cover the windows in black.
We cover them in black.

New York City Is the Capitol of the World

The babies burn
because the firetrucks
are out of water.

The mothers have run
away. The firemen
wait for water.

A young man was on
a roof before the firemen came,
with a camera.

He filmed the mothers run-
ning, the smoke, and
what looked like melting hands.

There are no men
more terrible than him,
but there are.

Frotteur

Stucco. Stucco. Stucco.
Your wife is gone, the kids sleep tight.

Portland cement, sand, and
mixed with a touch of lime grain—
What posture! She lets you plug things in her
sockets, lets you think you're tougher.

O what rubs tonight will see!
Windows stare: open jealousy.
When she fades you'll paint her new, an old
vertical lover to shield you from the cold.

She sees your worst but never turns
away. Rub, rub, stucco love! She firms
the house. She never cares what pace, never
gets enough. She lets you have your way with her

and have your way with her and have your way with her.
O wall, where should he touch you tonight?

Men's Room, Barnard

Girls live vespid.
They touch themselves

and are touched.
Girls tuck

their vaginas
in differently

each one
only to take

them out
again later.

The Man with No Children

has been told he should travel
to the ward of deep skin
grafts. People don't heal

says the man with no
children. How can they,
he says, when beasts make

rounds with names on
their tongues, lowering
dreamfulls of children into

the laps of the barren
who've sought late comfort
in parolees, cuddled

manslaughterers
who meant to
call it a night.

Radio: 4:01pm: 9 July

Leaving Church,
A Woman Is Attacked
With A Cement Block.

Derek Jeter
And The New York Yankees
Seek Revenge.

The Parkmoor Diner Has Fake Eggs

Hungrily I look at you
even when I don't
look at you. Only you eat fake eggs
so politely, love,
not one flustered vein

in your yoke, the decadence
of neon powder
settling easy like Sunday morning

in your belly,
which long ago decided
never to carry my child.

The Cop Who Rides Alone

passes rendezvous
in the park
and thinks about

parking, bores of
traffic
too easily

may
or may not
listen to self-

help tapes
considers getting a dog
calls for

backup
but never bleeds.
The cop who rides alone

is or appears to be
tougher
than the cop who needs

a partner
buddy with a matching
holster

a man to kick in doors for
with a comparably shiny
badge

a man to take
turns driving with
or bleed to

death on
whose eyes can't
heal but like saturated

tourniquets
do their best.

No One Eats in the Chinese Restaurants No One Eats In

The fish bloated, bonsai
overgrown, the bean curd

isn't what you'd expect
and they don't accept personal

checks. Behind the register,
Chinese sailors in a dragon

boat on the wall are not dressed
appropriately for sea, even low

tide. Are they blessed
by the dragon, does it stand

for something? Dear God in heaven,
what could take time

in a place like this, everything out
that won't go bad?

How long live wontons, dumplings
fried, the never-consumed

crab rangoons?

View from My Gym

At least one muscle of every machine
here malfunctions, take the bearing

ungreased, rustcovered nut, exhausted
tread, and the cooler, dead. Detectives are

jogging to my right and left, eight
miles each in half the time it takes to make

an arrest for driving under the influence.
I run and they run but we move forward

none, pounding our legs like a chopper
fleet in aerial support above the funnybone

junction of 195. The rookie detective to my right
asks the veteran detective to my left

if Nancy Ann, who he met last night at a marinara
gathering, is the daughter of Mayor Buddy Cianci:

*because if so that would make her Nancy Anne Cianci
—and is it true she has a fiancee?*

Gym shorts notwithstanding
they have me outnumbered, they have me

surrounded, but none bullhorn "We've got you
surrounded" so I keep on upping my revolutions

per minute, treadmill whining like an inmate's
first night. I bury my head in the bouncing

paper which says some ex-detective gets out today
and two more have been sentenced to three-to-five

for searing the penis of the man who slept with
the mayor's wife, for God knows how long,

with a cigarette, right down there on Benefit,
which is right down there in Providence.

Fools for the Danger of This Woman

go like hell for their guns.
Sirens rage on redlight streets.

Backup summoned. Officers
down. The whole damn town

ducks for cover from the white
of her eyes, the shock of her skin.

Don't nobody say a word,
warn the deputies.

Late night calls to fuck phones.
A million nine one ones.

Blood hair. Vinyl. Shades.
Get the rifle, son.

But don't look when you aim it.

for Erin

It Is Late But Not Too

Enough prayer in the wrong directions, God
in the definition of God
I hear you

looking, the window snow
does not melt
because I never move from it.

Unpleasantly, out of season, your husband,
like a noble process, still explains
what flowers do.
Still too—I believe this—you sleepwalk

here. The more you want the more
my amens are yours.

You Are Her New Lover

She loses her sun
dress on the floor
of the Angelika

theater as an F
train throttles and
throttles beneath us

I am the plastic
my seat is no arm
of a lover I have

been as if a train
I've put my head
down driven

as with a woman
made love to
by other men

one slips between
her legs
hoping to God

she'll love
what is done
to her.

Before You Marry Someone Else, in California

It's silly to cry into a fax machine
before I've even asked you to fly here
over the nervous winter nightfields
between us. I listen
through what you say to

Iowa maize popping
in the moonblaze of us
on either side.
Fly here.

There's a lunar eclipse
no one's remembering to
look up at. We'll
take off our clothes at the same time.
We'll look.

Reconsidering

After the quick, tired
glory, he stayed down

on the shoulder
of a pond and breathed in
the barren scent

of Leda, gone,
her shuddering done,
her thighs split

apart. The dew
still stuck to him,

indelible nectar.
There was an absence

in her glands, a shame
in him—he knew
he'd given more than

taken, but never gently.
After the air
was done being thick from him,

there was time.
He should have invited her

to sit on the grass
while he washed off in the water.

My Woman

That calm goddess
      swaying in sluggish opera
            is the Brooklyn Bridge's

titanic sleep
      sucked mute
            by a generator's izzzzzzzzzz—

and the F goes shackalack
      shackalackalackalackalack
            deaf and formal like a normal

mother the ferry wishes
      goodnight the water
            cobblestones might

as well be filled
      with those who love
            me I can't hear whatever

is dead and I can't see
      goes—. —. —.
            Tonight the air's

the perfume
      I was meant to wear
            all along the woman

for me the woman for me
      she waited five years
            the woman for me

will be here tomorrow.

We're Famous

We pretend we don't know
what eyes feel like
sunning us

stay in bed laughing
how physically close
two people need to be for one

to get inside the other
how silly your nose my
nose bumper to bumper

outside what blue minutia
the sky would be if we
chose to walk beneath her.

Everything Is Always About You

A Virginia from Eugene lives
in our house on Thursdays
I predicted she'd resemble Cathy
Bates in *Misery* but it turns out
Virginia's gothic with a smidgen
of Cameron Manheim and has hair
to her ass and a black trench coat
and a bag with spikes and says
abstract art has got to be "really
really" good to get *her* she's
also a "published writer" besides
being a "painter" and she's "not
thrilled with" her accommodations
though they cost her nothing I haven't
met her myself yet but her lips
are supposedly black even the
insides she says there are no
Jordanas in the art world so far
so no matter what her last name
becomes Jordana's got a leg up
and "should be grateful honey
do you know what I mean?"
how liberating to be Jordana paint
anything and people will know you
"more importantly remember you"
come to think of it are there any
Rosses out there yet maybe
Virginia will know I'll ask her.

I Love You During Dinner

The food is difficult,
café approximately
German, your wife-

to-be watching you
chew, sipping hard water
under pogromish lights,

and for the first time
you see a little
German in her.

If she said
ich liebe sie
what would you do?

Counter, with a grin,
ko hum ch
from the Polish

in you, offer
some *lubliu*
from the Russian?

Shh.
Just eat.

What to Do with the Ring

Nothing now a piece
of cake, beloved un-
gathered and now never
departing that dearly way

from airports past your radar
screen, the sky the way
it was before the ladies
came to throw you showers,

chuppah flat, a flag
to cover the known
soldier—one more question
before we leave all this:

What to do with
the wedding ring, now
that now, six weeks done,
one man gone, the man

you love is yours for good,
like January 8th, 1942:
your mother's father
gives this ring to

the face that matches
the woman's face
of a long lost dream
you know the dream

where a lover waits
five years to spend
the rest of her life
this ring around her

ready finger
like a promise
no one makes
you keep.

Telling

But what I keep from you I keep from me
you say and *this keeps me from you* unbathed
in swollen night I step out from the water
in tepid skin to shave this skin to pledge
in frigid air that *I am yours*, and now
I'll tell you everything I know.
All drunk on blood which thrombs in wake of you
I pulse—we're not the same—I dry.
I've died before and killed you too. A mouth
too shut can never taste a mouth too wide
cannot retreat the tongue from where it hides.

Alone in Our Place

Above us the city is
an awful mirror
wintering shards.

Your words, not yet
reflections, snow-
mark my lips:

the terror of you not
warm for our forty
Decembers. In our pine

the deathworms
undress our one body.
They start with you.

Signals

The emergency broadcast system
won't work people turn off radios
when the signal is sent that is a way
to get attention not help.

The dog behind the fence out my back window
fell sick last night in the garden and began
to howl when it couldn't get up I watched
for an hour watched heads fade back
away from windows blinds shut
watched the lights go out fall asleep.

Making Believe

I am pretending to be the one you have always loved,
next to you.

Fireskin knees bend,
embers tender the pink.

I am pretending to be the two of us
like buffalo moose
spreading folds, sifting fir.

We drink rum and we shudder.
You peel like a plum.
The walls dampen with musk heat.

It must be days now,
never leaving
but to bathe in woodbreeze,

squat down
and hide what we make.

Someone Says Draw You

Moonlit missing
children roam unrecognized

next to us on the street.
Look at their blue

faces:
you've become anonymous, too.

Our love matters
less than we'll ever

think: Our names
mean nothing. You are missing

everywhere the more your name:
nothing.

Someone says draw you: I draw
uneven a blue face.

Blame It on Division

Down on my knees again
I make you naked again
I hear the hair again

shudder, blink
stunned by tongue,
begging with flexes.

For the first time we are singing,
for the first time we are forgiven
for not speaking

words of division
—did we ever learn them?

We are coming
under single streams
growing deep.

Blame it on division
we come to such unions
wanting in our sleep.

Worship

the hammer
was ecstasy
in her hand:

    bent on his knees
    he looked up
    at the angel

Fourth Person

The unheard and
unheard of un-

referenced grammatically
unaccounted for which

cannot logically be
formed summoned near

or utilized and therefore is neither
present nor absent yet

suspended in the
ephemeral in which

we are all singular
in the plural. Sunk

beneath him her them
is this (   )

into which there is no
conjugation.

The fourth person
rests untongued

Dedications

I belong at the service,
flowers and tripwires,
a firefly prayer, so many
downed and didn't know it.

I belong with the ones
unknowing, whose celebrations
are always painted some past color
they can't make out.

Making Tea

Sweetgale,
I'm going to
look at you all day

again
tomorrow
perhaps all

your flower-
ing hours
look at you

fire in zero
gravity
will you burn out

before I
memorize
your thin leaves

I take back
the unnoticing
years

come
release your green
in foreverwater.

Dinoflagella

No one can say
if you're even
a plant

up to no good
in the green pondscum
as you wink

a ribless
nervous vein
young at your tip

no head
to lose no heart to
skip in your eager

mingling jerks
you don't open
your mouth you

don't have a
mouth but rub
and cuddle what

food you
snag from desmids
stonewarts

lily underbellies
you sneak up to
that don't know

you're there or
what you've come
to do just that

you're quick
busy
drunk on needs

mineral
seeds no head
to lose that

chlorophylled
work you do and
do and do.

A Fish

eats a fish
edits the meal
digests the prey's
stinging cells

allowing them to
its own surface
itself now
able to sting.

Blood
around wounds
soaks down
into pores.

But my cells
have not mingled
in the blood
of another phage.

In the pull
there is obligation
to live out these days
uncarried away.

If You Stood You Would Not Fall

Late, Sunday. Your soul
is bitter,
intoxicating
you say, but

I don't entirely
believe it. I think
many terrible things
happened. Men

said to you
things men
say, but you never
forgot them.

You are a
delicate maple
between
seasons.

What I would give
for you to rise
like a sleeping
tree, from

too many nights
outside the
small window
no one ever opened.

for Akhmatova

Have You Seen Me

You can't go a hundred in a sixty-five
on a highway you're not paying attention
to the troopers will gun you from behind
fake trees or hidden curves as a grassy
knoll slides down your eye's left side
like Evel Knievel's landing ramp but that's
exactly what I did and when I saw the trooper
I shot down to eighty but then back up
to a hundred when he started coming I took
the first exit onto a service road where
his car was too fast for my car he got me
the wind blew his hat onto my windshield
just keep a straight face got to keep
a straight face now he's out of his squad
car with a magnum light and that rifle
and I'm nothing to him but his bitch ex-wife
the screaming chief the IRS I shot his partner
fucked his girl I peed in his pancakes boiled
his rabbit spilled his cocaine there's a body
in my kitchen another in the bed I put brie
in them both to attract the rats I'm Happy
the Clown with a kid on my lap I'm Paul
Bernardo Patrick Bateman I go out at night
to dig up earthworms David Berkowitz
before his parking ticket I'm the man it takes
them careers to catch my face in banks
my name in the mouth of hungry dispatchers
cheekbones in the lead of composite sketchers
gait on the film of crossing guard eyes I've
lost this much hair put on this much weight
tattooed the text of APB's on the foreheads
of victims and when this trooper starts

asking me where I'm going so fast I'm going
to ask him where are any of us going officer
sir when it comes down to it aren't we all just
burning to put a face to a name.

Plants Move

Quiet,
like Amish,

prone
to air, given

the blue taste
of rain

in a green mouth
at night, muscling

in the day's
day like a cinematographer

reaching for blue
in a yellow drown,

her slow
neck

cleaves up, up, leaf,
leaf,

dreaming I must
go underground

to get anywhere
here, with my body

as it is, room for
room,

the slow hum
your prone heart

inching
closer

when I'm not
looking.

Naked Light Over Sleeping Water

Set these words
upon your heart

Teach them
to your children

When you lie down
and when you rise up...

magnolias
are the smell of

sun breathing
minerals.

The August song
of two lovers

does reach
the moon.

What is like you,
God?

To Heidegger

There are no seasons
between what is spoken

and what is not said: flower
and stone. There is talk of nihilism,

perpetual spiritual falling-
down, and soon burnt hair charcoals

the night. Moon's chilling
corona echoes breath on

Augen, and breath on ears,
and the sound of a woman's burning

eyes. The dead are dead
but somehow still they

seep crystalbreath,
       your ice witness.

after Paul Celan

Letter Home from Barcelona

It's still raining outside. I slice the melon's belly
for supper. The garlic roasts in the oven.
I won't say why I can't paint now, only that I can't
leave. And when I play old songs too loud
the neighbors toss potatoes through my windows.

Still I keep them open
and the drapes rain in.
My skin is not soft.

It's raining on the open market. The fat señoritas
all want to know what the red flower-fruit is.
I can't see well from here, but I tell them
raspberries: cook them with sugar and orange rinds.

Richard Lindner's Cast

To find symbols takes a certain personal investigation...
   —Lindner, 1977

1

The opposite of shaman is
one who deciphers souls
and extracts them,
who is not—as I'd like to think—
bad or insensitive.

2

I lived through so many introductions
today in the studio:
Ginsberg   gamblers   Louis II
extranjeros   robots   gunmen
prodigies   clowns   tigers
and Marilyn Monroe.

3

Nothing is ever quiet. Or makes more
sense. *Metropolis*
is not showing today
on any wall
but I hear it nonetheless.
You don't become American
in America.
I'm a tourist everywhere.

4

Back from Europe. Street people
eat people.
There were secret
smells, the pulsing corsets
of crepuscular women,
wild seductions,
skin liquors, open
trench coats,
all of which
I'm growing
to love
and paint.

My Eyes and Benicio del Toro's

below them
black adjectives
there's no word for

sockets in
the cancerwater
what's exotic comes from

under
so long
any light becomes the light

our gutterfull pits need
where pelts of our inner
wishing go

Poem for Míklos Radnóti

Has to do with the spot I stand
over the frail pale man with his raincoat on
several feet beneath me bunched up
like wood with a book of his poems
burning a hole in his chest wrapped in
death in his arms snuggled tight
without air in some ditch with the
dirt caked behind his ears he's

wishing he hadn't been so right
predicting the single shot
to the neck, falling
from line like a voice

shaking its head. He lay still,
told himself *Keep lying still* as if
arms next to him were pillows,
soft without pulse. The march

had been so long, each step one
shovel-load closer to the ditch,

guards checking for life,
wishing for someone to look at
him, stop.

Being Charles Nelson Reilly

I wish I was a sunbeam.
> —Charles Nelson Reilly on *Match Game*, NBC, 1973

I can tell Zsa Zsa Gabor's age
by counting her blanks. Call it a midlife
crisis, but when Zsa Zsa Gabor bought a hot
air balloon she needed hot air
to fill it up so she took it to

Dumb Donald is so dumb.
How dumb is he!
He's so dumb he thought his funny bone was his

Zsa Zsa Gabor often handles my blanky blank
and to be honest, it makes me feel like I'm

Dumb Donald is so dumb.
How dumb is he!
He's so dumb he took off all his blanks and started to

One time, Zsa Zsa Gabor stayed home sick from work
and I was so concerned, but before I called
the doctor I put my blank in her mouth.

Dumb Donald is so dumb.
How dumb is he?
He's so dumb he saw his shadow and thought it was

Zsa Zsa Gabor's blank
was so high, I rushed her immediately to

Dumb Donald is so dumb.
How dumb is he!
He's so dumb, he actually thought my blank had fallen off
    inside Zsa Zsa Gabor's

hot air balloons are pretty expensive these days,
you betcha, so when Zsa Zsa lost hers
over New Jersey the day she got sick,
she yelled at our blank blank like he was

Dumb Donald is so dumb.
How dumb is he!
He's really dumb.

The doctor asked her what the problem was and she said:
"Doctor, my lover the pretzel-maker has bad dreams. Often
I wake to find he's tied my blank in a knot."

"What's more," she said, "my previous lover, the driving
instructor,
used to tell me every night to blank the blank more blankly."

"Gosh," the doctor said, "what was growing up like
for you, Zsa Zsa Gabor?"

"When I was a little girl, I was left on a doorstep.
For years, I thought I was a blank."

Oh, and...

Where did the way lead when it led nowhere?
                      —Paul Celan

Several nights ago I realized
I've never suffered. I only
suffer because I am connected
to sufferers. Nothing
is necessary for me. Keeping house
comes easy. I leave well enough alone, tuck sheets of
rain into other sheets of

rain which came easy. When I sleep
I dream I drown.

I forgot to say:
Nothing is necessary to me but to do my duty.

Ossuary

The present arrangement
dates from 1870 and is the work of
Frantisek Rint. You can see his name
assembled on the wall over there; notice the bones
of forty-thousand are here.

      Something bleaches the eye
      indelibly.

Perhaps the most interesting arrangement, containing
at least one of each in the body, is
the chandelier in the center of the nave.

      A numen? Dilation
      of ache? A past color
      which cannot be made out?

Some, particularly the old, refuse
to come in, but outside

      an aura peacocks the night
      which is filled with nothing but
      a clarinet.

You Return from Your Daily Walk

I waited here waited
for what green thing
you'd come back
put in my hand
examine my face compared to.

Last night the tip of me
as we stared it down went
numb in your fingers
like my sister
dreaming itself
empty of itself.

I'm here
you see I'm here
you wanted me naked to return to
climb into bed with but
all I am is an aftershock
of my quiet detonations.

This book is set in a Garamond typeface based upon the original
Garamond set, which was designed in the sixteenth century by
printer and publisher Claude Garamond. Garamond's types were
fashioned after those used by Venetian printers at the end of the
fifteenth century. The Garamond italics in this book are modeled
after types designed by Robert Granjon, a contemporary
of Garamond's.